# ADVANCED

# MACD

## Indicator

by

Lalit Mohanty

# PREFACE

The concept of MACD has been a cornerstone in technical analysis since its inception. Over the years, traders have embraced MACD for its ability to capture momentum, identify trends, and generate timely buy and sell signals. In this book, we embark on a journey through the intricate landscape of MACD, unraveling its various components and unveiling the multitude of strategies it offers.

The book is divided into 25 chapters, each meticulously crafted to cover different facets of MACD trading. We start with the basics, ensuring a solid understanding of MACD components and their interpretation. As you progress through the chapters, you will delve into both fundamental and advanced MACD strategies, gaining insights into trend identification, crossovers, divergence, convergence, and much more.

Throughout the book, we emphasize practical application, providing real-world examples, case studies, and insights into potential pitfalls. We also explore how MACD can be integrated with other technical analysis tools, offering a holistic approach to market analysis.

In the later chapters, we venture into more advanced topics such as MACD customization, automation, and its application in specific markets like cryptocurrencies. The goal is not only to equip you with a deep understanding of MACD but also to empower you to adapt and evolve your strategies to changing market conditions.

# Table of Contents

- Understanding the relationship between MACD and market volatility

- Adjusting strategies for high and low volatility environments

## Chapter 14: MACD and Fibonacci Retracements

- Integrating MACD with Fibonacci retracement levels

- Combining two powerful tools for precise entries and exits

## Chapter 15: MACD and Elliott Wave Theory

- Harmonizing MACD with Elliott Wave patterns

- Enhancing wave counting and trend identification

## Chapter 16: MACD and Sector Rotation

- Using MACD to identify sector trends

- Rotating positions based on sector strength

## Chapter 17: Statistical Analysis of MACD Strategies

- Backtesting MACD strategies

- Evaluating performance and risk metrics

## Chapter 18: Automation with MACD

- Creating and implementing MACD-based trading algorithms

- Incorporating automation for efficiency

## Chapter 19: MACD in Options Trading

- Leveraging MACD for options strategies

- Hedging and risk management with MACD

## Chapter 20: Psychological Aspects of MACD Trading

- Managing emotions while trading with MACD

- Developing discipline and patience

## Chapter 21: Real-world Examples

- Case studies of successful MACD trades

- Learning from both wins and losses

## Chapter 22: Common Mistakes in MACD Trading

- Identifying and avoiding pitfalls

- Fine-tuning strategies for better results

## Chapter 23: MACD in Cryptocurrency Trading

- Adapting MACD to the cryptocurrency market

- Strategies for trading digital assets

## Chapter 24: Future Developments in MACD

- Recent advancements in MACD analysis

- Potential future innovations and improvements

## Chapter 25: Conclusion

- Summarizing key takeaways

- Encouraging ongoing learning and adaptation

# CHAPTER 1

# INTRODUCTION TO MACD

Moving Average Convergence Divergence (MACD) stands as one of the most popular and versatile indicators in the realm of technical analysis. Developed by Gerald Appel in the late 1970s, MACD has since become a staple tool for traders across various financial markets. In this chapter, we delve into the fundamentals of MACD, understanding its components and how it operates.

## What is MACD?

At its core, MACD is a trend-following momentum indicator that provides insights into the strength and direction of a trend. It achieves this by analyzing the relationship between two moving averages of an asset's price. The interaction between these moving averages generates signals that traders use to make informed trading decisions.

## Components of MACD:

**1. MACD Line:** The MACD line represents the difference between two exponential moving averages (EMAs). Typically, these EMAs are calculated over different time periods, commonly 12 and 26 periods. The formula to calculate the MACD line is:

MACD Line = 12-period EMA - 26-period EMA

The resulting line oscillates around the zero line, with positive values indicating that the short-term EMA is above the long-term EMA, suggesting bullish momentum, while negative values suggest bearish momentum.

**2. Signal Line:** The signal line, also known as the trigger line, is a smoothed version of the MACD line. It is calculated by taking the exponential moving average of the MACD line itself, commonly over a 9-period timeframe. The signal line helps to smooth out the MACD line's fluctuations, providing clearer buy and sell signals.

**3. Histogram:** The histogram is derived from the difference between the MACD line and the signal line. It provides a visual representation of the divergence/convergence between these two lines. When the MACD line is above the signal line, the histogram is positive, indicating bullish momentum. Conversely, when the MACD line is below the signal line, the histogram is negative, suggesting bearish momentum.

**Interpretation of MACD:**

- **Crossovers:** One of the primary ways traders use MACD is by observing crossovers between the MACD line and the signal line. A bullish crossover occurs when the MACD line crosses above the signal line, signaling a potential uptrend. Conversely, a bearish crossover occurs when the MACD line crosses below the signal line, signaling a potential downtrend.

- **Divergence and Convergence:** MACD divergence and convergence occur when the MACD line diverges or converges with the price action of the underlying asset. Bullish divergence occurs when the price makes lower lows while the

MACD line forms higher lows, indicating potential bullish reversal. Conversely, bearish divergence occurs when the price makes higher highs while the MACD line forms lower highs, suggesting potential bearish reversal.

In summary, MACD is a powerful tool for analyzing trend direction, momentum, and potential reversal points in financial markets. By understanding its components and interpreting its signals, traders can gain valuable insights to enhance their trading decisions. In the following chapters, we will explore various MACD strategies in depth, empowering traders to harness the full potential of this versatile indicator.

# CHAPTER 2

# HISTORICAL PERSPECTIVE

**Origins and Development of MACD:**

The Moving Average Convergence Divergence (MACD) indicator, conceived by Gerald Appel in the late 1970s, emerged during a time of burgeoning interest in technical analysis tools. Appel, a seasoned trader and analyst, sought to develop a dynamic indicator that could effectively capture both momentum and trend direction in financial markets.

The concept behind MACD was rooted in the convergence and divergence of two exponential moving averages (EMAs) of an asset's price. By comparing shorter-term and longer-term EMAs, MACD aimed to provide traders with insights into the strength and direction of prevailing trends. The initial version of MACD utilized a 12-period EMA and a 26-period EMA, with the difference between these two lines serving as the primary signal.

Over time, MACD underwent refinements and adaptations to enhance its effectiveness and versatility. Traders and analysts experimented with different settings, such as altering the periods of the EMAs or introducing additional smoothing components. These modifications aimed to fine-tune MACD's sensitivity to market movements and improve its ability to generate accurate signals.

**Evolution of MACD in Trading Strategies:**

Since its inception, MACD has played a pivotal role in a wide array of trading strategies across various financial markets. Its simplicity and versatility have made it a favorite among traders of all experience levels, from novices to seasoned professionals.

In the early days, MACD was primarily used as a trend-following indicator, with traders relying on crossovers between the MACD line and its signal line to identify entry and exit points. Bullish crossovers, where the MACD line crosses above the signal line, signaled potential buying opportunities, while bearish crossovers, where the MACD line crosses below the signal line, indicated potential selling opportunities.

As traders gained familiarity with MACD, they began to explore more advanced applications of the indicator. Strategies incorporating MACD divergence and convergence emerged, leveraging the divergence between the MACD line and price action to identify potential trend reversals. Bullish divergence, where the price forms lower lows while the MACD line forms higher lows, signaled potential bullish reversals, while bearish divergence, where the price forms higher highs while the MACD line forms lower highs, signaled potential bearish reversals.

Additionally, MACD found utility in conjunction with other technical analysis tools, such as moving averages, support and resistance levels, and chart patterns. By integrating MACD with complementary indicators, traders could enhance the accuracy and reliability of their trading signals, leading to more profitable outcomes.

In recent years, with the advent of algorithmic trading and quantitative analysis, MACD has continued to evolve. Traders have developed sophisticated algorithms and trading systems that incorporate MACD as a key component, automating the process of signal generation and trade execution. This automation has allowed traders to capitalize on the speed and efficiency of computerized trading, enabling them to execute trades with precision and consistency.

Overall, the historical evolution of MACD reflects its enduring popularity and effectiveness as a technical analysis tool. From its humble beginnings as a simple trend-following indicator to its role in sophisticated algorithmic trading systems, MACD has remained a cornerstone of trading strategies, standing the test of time in an ever-changing market landscape. In the subsequent chapters, we will explore various MACD strategies in detail, equipping traders with the knowledge and skills to leverage this powerful indicator to its fullest potential.

# CHAPTER 3

# BASIC MACD SETUP

Moving Average Convergence Divergence (MACD) is a versatile technical indicator that can be easily incorporated into charting platforms to assist traders in analyzing market trends and momentum. In this chapter, we will discuss the basic setup of MACD on charts and how to interpret its signals effectively.

**Setting up MACD on Charts:**

Setting up MACD on most charting platforms is a straightforward process. Here's a step-by-step guide:

1. **Open a Chart:** Begin by selecting the financial instrument or asset you want to analyze. This could be a stock, currency pair, commodity, or any other tradable asset.

2. **Add MACD Indicator:** Look for the option to add indicators or overlays on your charting platform. Find MACD among the list of available indicators and add it to your chart.

3. **Adjust Settings (Optional):** By default, MACD is typically configured with a 12-period and 26-period exponential moving average (EMA), along with a 9-period EMA for the signal line. However, some traders may prefer different settings based on their trading style and preferences. You can adjust the settings to customize the indicator according to your needs.

4. **Apply the Indicator:** Once you have configured the settings, apply the MACD indicator to your chart. You should now see the MACD line, signal line, and histogram plotted on the chart.

**Interpretation of MACD Signals:**

Now that you have set up MACD on your chart, let's discuss how to interpret its signals:

1. **MACD Line (Blue Line):** The MACD line represents the difference between the 12-period and 26-period EMAs. When the MACD line is above the zero line, it indicates that the short-term EMA is above the long-term EMA, suggesting bullish momentum. Conversely, when the MACD line is below the zero line, it suggests bearish momentum.

2. **Signal Line (Orange Line):** The signal line is a 9-period EMA of the MACD line. It helps to smooth out the MACD line's fluctuations and generates trading signals. When the MACD line crosses above the signal line, it generates a bullish signal, indicating a potential buying opportunity. Conversely, when the MACD line crosses below the signal line, it generates a bearish signal, indicating a potential selling opportunity.

3. **Histogram:** The histogram represents the difference between the MACD line and the signal line. It provides a visual representation of the divergence/convergence between these two lines. When the histogram is above the zero line and increasing in height, it suggests increasing bullish momentum.

Conversely, when the histogram is below the zero line and decreasing in height, it suggests increasing bearish momentum.

**Interpreting MACD Crossovers:**

One of the most common ways to interpret MACD signals is through crossovers between the MACD line and the signal line. Here's how to interpret these crossovers:

- **Bullish Crossover:** When the MACD line crosses above the signal line, it generates a bullish crossover signal. This suggests that the bullish momentum is strengthening, and it may be a good time to consider entering a long position.

- **Bearish Crossover:** Conversely, when the MACD line crosses below the signal line, it generates a bearish crossover signal. This suggests that the bearish momentum is strengthening, and it may be a good time to consider entering a short position or closing long positions.

In summary, setting up MACD on charts is a simple process that can provide valuable insights into market trends and momentum. By interpreting MACD signals effectively, traders can make informed trading decisions and capitalize on potential opportunities in the market. In the following chapters, we will explore various MACD trading strategies in more detail, helping traders to harness the full potential of this powerful indicator.

# CHAPTER 4

# TREND IDENTIFICATION WITH MACD

Moving Average Convergence Divergence (MACD) is a powerful tool not only for spotting trends but also for confirming their direction and strength. In this chapter, we will explore how MACD can be used to identify trend direction and recognize different market phases.

**Recognizing Trend Direction using MACD:**

Trend identification is a fundamental aspect of technical analysis, as trends provide valuable insights into the overall market sentiment and can guide trading decisions. MACD offers several methods for recognizing trend direction:

1. **MACD Line and Signal Line Relationship:** The relationship between the MACD line and the signal line can provide clues about the prevailing trend. When the MACD line is above the signal line, it suggests bullish momentum and indicates an uptrend. Conversely, when the MACD line is below the signal line, it suggests bearish momentum and indicates a downtrend.

2. **MACD Histogram:** The histogram, which represents the difference between the MACD line and the signal line, can also help identify trend direction. A positive histogram indicates that the MACD line is above the signal line and suggests bullish momentum, while a negative histogram indicates bearish momentum.

3. **MACD Slope:** Observing the slope of the MACD line can further confirm trend direction. A rising MACD line suggests increasing bullish momentum and a strengthening uptrend, while a declining MACD line suggests increasing bearish momentum and a strengthening downtrend.

By analyzing these aspects of MACD, traders can gain a clearer understanding of the prevailing trend and make more informed trading decisions.

**Identifying Market Phases with MACD+**

In addition to identifying trend direction, MACD can also be used to recognize different market phases, including consolidation, expansion, and contraction. The "MACD+" approach incorporates additional components to provide a more comprehensive analysis of market dynamics:

1. **Consolidation Phase:** During periods of consolidation, where the market is range-bound and lacks a clear trend, the MACD histogram tends to oscillate around the zero line, and the MACD line and signal line may converge. Traders may interpret this as a signal to stand aside and avoid trading until a clear trend emerges.

2. **Expansion Phase:** In an expansion phase, where the market experiences a strong trend, the MACD histogram tends to diverge from the zero line, and the MACD line and signal line may diverge as well. Traders may interpret this as a signal to

enter trades in the direction of the trend, as momentum is strong and likely to continue.

3. **Contraction Phase:** During periods of contraction, where the market experiences a weakening trend or transitions from an expansion phase to a consolidation phase, the MACD histogram may fluctuate around the zero line, and the MACD line and signal line may converge. Traders may interpret this as a signal to reduce exposure and tighten stop-loss levels, as the market may be preparing for a reversal or extended consolidation.

By incorporating these additional components into the analysis, traders can gain a deeper understanding of market dynamics and adapt their strategies accordingly.

# CHAPTER 5

# MACD CROSSOVERS

Moving Average Convergence Divergence (MACD) crossovers are among the most widely used signals by traders to identify potential trend reversals and entry/exit points. In this chapter, we will delve into the intricacies of MACD crossovers, including their interpretation and implementation in trading strategies.

**Understanding MACD Crossovers:**

MACD crossovers occur when the MACD line crosses above or below the signal line, signaling a shift in momentum and potentially the beginning of a new trend. There are two types of MACD crossovers: bullish crossovers and bearish crossovers.

1. **Bullish Crossover:** A bullish crossover occurs when the MACD line crosses above the signal line. This indicates that the short-term EMA (12-period) has crossed above the longer-term EMA (26-period), suggesting strengthening bullish momentum. Traders interpret this crossover as a signal to enter long positions or as confirmation of an existing uptrend.

2. **Bearish Crossover:** Conversely, a bearish crossover occurs when the MACD line crosses below the signal line. This indicates that the short-term EMA has crossed below the longer-term EMA, suggesting strengthening bearish momentum. Traders interpret this crossover as a signal to enter short positions or as confirmation of an existing downtrend.

**Bullish and Bearish Crossover Strategies:**

Trading strategies based on MACD crossovers typically involve the following steps:

1. **Identify Potential Crossover:** Monitor the MACD line and signal line for potential crossovers. Look for instances where the MACD line approaches or crosses above/below the signal line.

2. **Confirm with Price Action:** Before executing a trade based on a crossover signal, it's important to confirm the signal with price action. Look for additional evidence such as support/resistance levels, chart patterns, or candlestick formations that align with the crossover signal.

3. **Entry Point:** Once a crossover signal is confirmed, determine your entry point. For bullish crossovers, consider entering a long position either immediately after the crossover or on a pullback to support levels. For bearish crossovers, consider entering a short position either immediately after the crossover or on a bounce to resistance levels.

4. **Set Stop-Loss and Take-Profit Levels:** To manage risk, set stop-loss orders to limit potential losses in case the trade goes against you. Take-profit orders can be set to lock in profits once the trade moves in your favor.

5. **Monitor Trade:** Continuously monitor the trade after entry. Adjust stop-loss and take-profit levels as needed based on market conditions and price action.

6. **Exit Strategy:** Determine your exit strategy before entering the trade. This could involve exiting the trade when the MACD line crosses back over the signal line in the opposite direction or when price reaches a predetermined target.

**Conclusion:**

MACD crossovers provide valuable signals for identifying potential trend reversals and entry/exit points in the market. By understanding the dynamics of bullish and bearish crossovers and implementing appropriate trading strategies, traders can capitalize on opportunities and improve their trading outcomes. However, it's essential to combine MACD crossovers with other technical analysis tools and consider market context to enhance the effectiveness of these signals. In the subsequent chapters, we will explore advanced MACD strategies and techniques to further optimize trading performance.

# CHAPTER 6

# MACD HISTOGRAM STRATEGIES

The MACD histogram, derived from the difference between the MACD line and the signal line, provides valuable insights into the momentum and strength of a trend. In this chapter, we will delve into the interpretation of the MACD histogram and explore various trading strategies based on histogram patterns.

**Interpreting MACD Histogram:**

The MACD histogram serves as a visual representation of the divergence or convergence between the MACD line and the signal line. Understanding the histogram's patterns and movements can help traders gauge the momentum and potential direction of the market.

1. **Positive Histogram:** A positive histogram occurs when the MACD line is above the signal line, indicating bullish momentum. The height of the histogram bars reflects the strength of the bullish momentum. Increasing histogram bars suggest strengthening bullish momentum, while decreasing bars indicate weakening momentum.

2. **Negative Histogram:** Conversely, a negative histogram occurs when the MACD line is below the signal line, indicating bearish momentum. Similar to a positive histogram, the height of the histogram bars reflects the strength of the bearish momentum. Increasing negative histogram bars suggest strengthening bearish momentum, while decreasing bars indicate weakening momentum.

3. **Zero Line Crossings:** Zero line crossings of the histogram can also provide important signals. When the histogram crosses above the zero line from negative to positive, it indicates a shift from bearish to bullish momentum, signaling a potential uptrend. Conversely, when the histogram crosses below the zero line from positive to negative, it indicates a shift from bullish to bearish momentum, signaling a potential downtrend.

**Trading Strategies Based on Histogram Patterns:**

Several trading strategies can be implemented based on the patterns and movements of the MACD histogram:

1. **Histogram Divergence:** Histogram divergence occurs when the histogram forms higher highs or lower lows while price action forms opposite patterns. Bullish histogram divergence, where the histogram forms higher highs while price forms lower lows, suggests potential bullish reversal. Conversely, bearish histogram divergence, where the histogram forms lower lows while price forms higher highs, suggests potential bearish reversal.

2. **Histogram Convergence:** Histogram convergence occurs when the histogram aligns with price action, confirming the strength of the prevailing trend. Bullish histogram convergence, where the histogram forms higher highs along with rising prices, confirms bullish momentum. Conversely, bearish histogram convergence, where the histogram forms

lower lows along with falling prices, confirms bearish momentum.

3. **Histogram Patterns:** Traders can also analyze specific patterns formed by the histogram, such as double tops, double bottoms, and head and shoulders formations. These patterns can provide valuable signals for trend reversals or continuation.

4. **Histogram Momentum:** Traders can use the height and direction of histogram bars to gauge momentum. A series of increasing histogram bars suggests strengthening momentum in the direction of the trend, while decreasing bars suggest weakening momentum and potential trend reversal.

# CHAPTER 7

# DIVERGENCE AND CONVERGENCE

Moving Average Convergence Divergence (MACD) divergence and convergence are powerful signals used by traders to identify potential trend reversals and continuation patterns. In this chapter, we will delve into the concept of divergence and convergence on MACD and explore trading strategies based on these signals.

**Spotting Divergence and Convergence on MACD:**

Divergence and convergence occur when the MACD line diverges or converges with the price action of the underlying asset. These phenomena can provide valuable insights into the underlying strength or weakness of a trend.

1. **Bullish Divergence:** Bullish divergence occurs when the price forms lower lows while the MACD line forms higher lows. This suggests that while the price is declining, momentum on the MACD indicator is shifting upwards, indicating potential bullish reversal.

2. **Bearish Divergence:** Conversely, bearish divergence occurs when the price forms higher highs while the MACD line forms lower highs. This suggests that while the price is rising, momentum on the MACD indicator is weakening, indicating potential bearish reversal.

3. **Bullish Convergence:** Bullish convergence occurs when the price forms higher highs while the MACD line also forms higher highs. This confirms the strength of the prevailing uptrend, as both price and momentum are moving in the same direction.

4. **Bearish Convergence:** Similarly, bearish convergence occurs when the price forms lower lows while the MACD line also forms lower lows. This confirms the strength of the prevailing downtrend, as both price and momentum are moving in the same direction.

**Trading Reversal Signals with Divergence/Convergence:**

Trading strategies based on MACD divergence and convergence typically involve the following steps:

1. **Identify Divergence/Convergence:** Monitor the price action and MACD indicator for signs of divergence or convergence. Look for instances where the price and MACD line move in opposite directions, indicating potential reversal signals.

2. **Confirm with Price Action:** Before executing a trade based on divergence or convergence signals, confirm the signal with price action. Look for additional evidence such as support/resistance levels, chart patterns, or candlestick formations that align with the divergence/convergence signal.

3. **Entry Point:** Once a divergence or convergence signal is confirmed, determine your entry point. For bullish divergence, consider entering a long position either immediately after the

divergence signal or on a pullback to support levels. For bearish divergence, consider entering a short position either immediately after the divergence signal or on a bounce to resistance levels.

4. **Set Stop-Loss and Take-Profit Levels:** To manage risk, set stop-loss orders to limit potential losses in case the trade goes against you. Take-profit orders can be set to lock in profits once the trade moves in your favor.

5. **Monitor Trade:** Continuously monitor the trade after entry. Adjust stop-loss and take-profit levels as needed based on market conditions and price action.

6. **Exit Strategy:** Determine your exit strategy before entering the trade. This could involve exiting the trade when the MACD line converges with price action in the opposite direction or when price reaches a predetermined target.

# CHAPTER 8

# MACD AND PRICE ACTION

Integrating Moving Average Convergence Divergence (MACD) with price action analysis can provide traders with a robust framework for making informed trading decisions. In this chapter, we will explore how MACD can be effectively combined with other technical analysis tools to confirm price action signals and enhance trading strategies.

**Integrating MACD with Other Technical Analysis Tools:**

MACD is often used in conjunction with other technical indicators to validate trading signals and strengthen analysis. Some commonly used technical analysis tools that can be integrated with MACD include:

1. **Support and Resistance Levels:** Support and resistance levels are key areas on a price chart where buying and selling pressure converge. MACD can be used to confirm breaks above resistance or below support levels, providing additional validation for potential trend reversals or continuations.

2. **Moving Averages:** Moving averages are trend-following indicators that smooth out price data over a specified period. Traders often use MACD in combination with moving averages to identify trend direction and potential entry/exit points. For example, a bullish crossover of the MACD line above the signal line, accompanied by price trading above a rising moving average, can signal a strong uptrend.

3. **Chart Patterns:** Chart patterns, such as triangles, flags, and head and shoulders formations, are visual representations of price movements that can help traders anticipate future price action. MACD can be used to confirm the validity of chart patterns by analyzing whether divergence or convergence signals align with the pattern's breakout or breakdown.

4. **Volume Analysis:** Volume is an essential component of price action analysis, as it provides insights into the strength and conviction of market participants. Traders can use MACD in conjunction with volume analysis to confirm the significance of price moves. For example, a bullish divergence signal on MACD accompanied by increasing volume suggests strong buying pressure and validates a potential trend reversal.

**Using MACD to Confirm Price Action Signals:**

MACD can also be used to confirm price action signals and validate trading decisions. Some ways in which MACD can confirm price action signals include:

1. **Divergence/Convergence Confirmation:** MACD divergence or convergence signals can confirm the validity of price action patterns, such as double tops/bottoms or head and shoulders formations. For example, a bullish divergence signal on MACD accompanying a double bottom pattern strengthens the bullish reversal signal.

2. **Trend Confirmation:** MACD can confirm the strength and direction of a trend identified through price action analysis. For instance, if price breaks out above a resistance level and MACD also shows a bullish crossover, it provides confirmation of the uptrend and reinforces the bullish bias.

3. **Reversal Confirmation:** MACD divergence or convergence signals can confirm potential trend reversals identified through price action analysis. Traders can use MACD to validate reversal patterns such as engulfing candles or hammer candles, increasing the probability of successful trades.

# CHAPTER 9

# MACD AND MOVING AVERAGES

Moving Average Convergence Divergence (MACD) is often used in conjunction with various types of moving averages to enhance trend-following strategies and improve trading outcomes. In this chapter, we will explore how MACD can be effectively combined with different moving averages to identify trends and generate reliable trading signals.

**Combining MACD with Different Moving Averages:**

MACD can be combined with different types of moving averages, including simple moving averages (SMA) and exponential moving averages (EMA), to provide additional confirmation of trend direction and strength. Here are some common combinations:

1. **MACD with SMA:** Combining MACD with SMA can help smooth out price fluctuations and provide clearer trend signals. For example, traders may use a 50-period SMA in conjunction with MACD to confirm the direction of the primary trend. A bullish crossover of the MACD line above the signal line, accompanied

by price trading above the 50-period SMA, may signal a strong uptrend.

2. **MACD with EMA:** EMA responds more quickly to recent price data compared to SMA, making it a popular choice for trend-following strategies. Traders often use a shorter-term EMA (e.g., 9-period) and a longer-term EMA (e.g., 21-period) in conjunction with MACD to identify trend changes. A bullish crossover of the MACD line above the signal line, along with price trading above both the 9-period and 21-period EMA, may confirm a bullish trend reversal.

3. **MACD Histogram with Moving Average Crossovers:** Traders can also use the MACD histogram in conjunction with moving average crossovers to confirm trend strength. For example, a bullish crossover of the MACD line above the signal line, accompanied by a positive histogram and price trading above a rising moving average, may provide strong confirmation of an uptrend.

**Enhancing Trend-Following Strategies:**

Combining MACD with moving averages can enhance trend-following strategies in the following ways:

1. **Confirmation of Trend Direction:** By using MACD in conjunction with moving averages, traders can confirm the direction of the prevailing trend. A bullish crossover of the MACD line above the signal line, accompanied by price trading above a rising moving average, provides strong confirmation of an uptrend.

2. **Identification of Trend Reversals:** MACD can help identify potential trend reversals when used in combination with moving averages. Traders may look for bearish crossovers of the MACD line below the signal line, accompanied by price

trading below a declining moving average, to signal a potential downtrend reversal.

3. **Filtering Out False Signals:** Moving averages can act as filters to help traders distinguish between genuine trend signals and false signals. By requiring confirmation from both MACD and moving averages, traders can reduce the likelihood of entering trades based on temporary price fluctuations.

# CHAPTER 10

# MACD AND SUPPORT/RESISTANCE

Incorporating Moving Average Convergence Divergence (MACD) with support and resistance analysis can provide traders with a comprehensive framework for identifying key price levels and trading breakouts and breakdowns. In this chapter, we will explore how MACD can be utilized to identify support and resistance levels and confirm breakout and breakdown signals.

**Utilizing MACD to Identify Key Support and Resistance Levels:**

Support and resistance levels are crucial areas on a price chart where buying and selling pressure converge. MACD can be used to identify these levels and provide confirmation of their significance. Here's how:

1. **Price Consolidation:** During periods of price consolidation, where the market is range-bound and lacks a clear trend, MACD can help identify key support and resistance levels. Traders can look for instances where the MACD histogram oscillates around the zero line, indicating that the market is in

a state of equilibrium. Support and resistance levels can be identified based on previous price peaks and troughs, and MACD can provide confirmation of these levels by showing convergence or divergence with price action.

2. **Trend Confirmation:** When the market is trending, support and resistance levels can act as dynamic areas where price may pause or reverse. MACD can be used to confirm the validity of these levels by analyzing whether divergence or convergence signals align with support and resistance zones. For example, a bullish divergence signal on MACD accompanying a bounce off a support level strengthens the bullish bias and confirms the significance of the support level.

## Trading Breakouts and Breakdowns with MACD Confirmation:

Breakouts and breakdowns occur when price moves decisively above or below a key support or resistance level, signaling a potential change in trend direction. MACD can be used to confirm these signals and provide additional validation for trading decisions. Here's how:

1. **Breakout Confirmation:** When price breaks out above a resistance level, traders can look for confirmation from MACD to validate the breakout. A bullish crossover of the MACD line above the signal line, accompanied by increasing bullish momentum on the histogram, provides confirmation of the breakout and strengthens the bullish bias.

2. **Breakdown Confirmation:** Conversely, when price breaks down below a support level, traders can use MACD to confirm the breakdown. A bearish crossover of the MACD line below the signal line, accompanied by increasing bearish momentum on the histogram, provides confirmation of the breakdown and strengthens the bearish bias.

## Key Considerations:

- **Volume Confirmation:** Volume analysis can further validate breakout and breakdown signals. Traders can look for increasing volume on breakout/breakdown candles to confirm the strength of the move.

- **Price Rejection:** MACD can also help identify instances of price rejection at key support and resistance levels. Divergence or convergence signals on MACD, accompanied by rejection wicks or reversal candlestick patterns, provide additional confirmation of the significance of these levels.

# CHAPTER 11

# MULTIPLE TIME FRAME ANALYSIS WITH MACD

Multiple Time Frame Analysis (MTFA) is a powerful approach used by traders to gain a comprehensive view of the market by analyzing price action across different timeframes. In this chapter, we will explore how Moving Average Convergence Divergence (MACD) can be applied to multiple timeframes and how aligning signals across these timeframes can lead to better trading accuracy.

**Applying MACD on Different Timeframes:**

MACD can be applied to various timeframes, ranging from intraday charts to longer-term charts, to capture different aspects of price action and market trends. By analyzing MACD signals across multiple timeframes, traders can gain deeper insights into the overall market dynamics. Here's how MACD can be applied on different timeframes:

1. **Intraday Charts (e.g., 5-minute, 15-minute):** On intraday charts, MACD can help traders identify short-term trends and

trading opportunities. Traders may use shorter-term settings for MACD, such as 5-period and 13-period EMAs, to capture rapid price movements and intraday trends.

2. **Hourly and Daily Charts:** On hourly and daily charts, MACD can help traders identify medium-term trends and potential swing trading opportunities. Traders may use intermediate-term settings for MACD, such as 12-period and 26-period EMAs, to capture trends that unfold over several days or weeks.

3. **Weekly and Monthly Charts:** On weekly and monthly charts, MACD can help traders identify long-term trends and investment opportunities. Traders may use longer-term settings for MACD, such as 26-period and 52-period EMAs, to capture trends that develop over several months or years.

## Aligning Signals for Better Accuracy:

Aligning MACD signals across different timeframes can provide confirmation and validation of trading signals, leading to better accuracy in trading decisions. Here's how traders can align signals across multiple timeframes:

1. **Confirming Trend Direction:** Traders can use MACD signals on higher timeframes to confirm the direction of the prevailing trend. For example, if MACD on the daily chart shows a bullish crossover, traders may look for bullish signals on shorter timeframes, such as the 4-hour chart, to enter trades in the direction of the trend.

2. **Identifying Entry and Exit Points:** Traders can use MACD signals on multiple timeframes to identify optimal entry and exit points. For example, if MACD on the daily chart shows a bullish crossover, traders may wait for a pullback on the 1-

hour chart and look for bullish reversal signals to enter trades at lower risk levels.

3. **Validating Reversal Signals:** Traders can use MACD signals on multiple timeframes to validate reversal signals and avoid false signals. For example, if MACD on the daily chart shows a bearish divergence, traders may wait for confirmation from MACD on the 4-hour chart before entering trades, increasing the probability of success.

## Key Considerations:

- **Timeframe Selection:** Traders should choose a combination of timeframes that suit their trading style and objectives. For example, day traders may focus on shorter timeframes, while swing traders may use a combination of shorter and longer timeframes.

- **Consistency:** Traders should maintain consistency in their analysis across different timeframes to avoid confusion and ensure coherence in their trading decisions.

# CHAPTER 12

# ADVANCED MACD SETTINGS

Moving Average Convergence Divergence (MACD) is a versatile technical indicator that can be customized with various settings to adapt to specific market conditions and trading preferences. In this chapter, we will explore alternative MACD settings and discuss how traders can adapt MACD to different market environments for more effective analysis.

**Exploring Alternative MACD Settings:**

While the default MACD settings (12-period and 26-period exponential moving averages with a 9-period signal line) are widely used, traders can experiment with alternative settings to suit their trading style and objectives. Here are some alternative MACD settings to consider:

1. **Shorter-term Settings:** Traders looking for more responsive signals may opt for shorter-term settings for MACD. For example, using a 5-period and 10-period exponential moving average for the MACD line and a 5-period signal line can

generate faster signals, suitable for intraday trading or capturing short-term price movements.

2. **Longer-term Settings:** Conversely, traders with a longer-term perspective may prefer longer-term settings for MACD to filter out noise and focus on broader trends. For example, using a 20-period and 50-period exponential moving average for the MACD line and a 10-period signal line can provide smoother signals, suitable for swing trading or trend-following strategies.

3. **Customized Settings:** Traders can also experiment with customized settings for MACD based on their analysis and preferences. For example, adjusting the parameters of the MACD line, signal line, or histogram can fine-tune the sensitivity of the indicator and adapt it to specific market conditions.

**Adapting MACD to Specific Market Conditions:**

MACD can be adapted to different market conditions, including trending markets, ranging markets, and volatile markets, by adjusting the settings and interpretation of the indicator. Here's how traders can adapt MACD to specific market conditions:

1. **Trending Markets:** In trending markets, MACD can be used to identify the direction and strength of the trend. Traders may focus on MACD crossovers and histogram expansion for trend confirmation and continuation signals. Using longer-term settings for MACD can help smooth out noise and capture broader trends in trending markets.

2. **Ranging Markets:** In ranging markets, where price moves within a defined range, MACD can be used to identify support and resistance levels and potential breakout or breakdown points. Traders may look for convergence and divergence

signals on MACD to anticipate trend reversals at key price levels.

3. **Volatile Markets:** In volatile markets, MACD can help traders navigate price fluctuations and identify potential trend changes. Traders may use shorter-term settings for MACD to capture rapid price movements and adapt quickly to changing market conditions.

## Key Considerations:

- **Backtesting:** Before using alternative MACD settings in live trading, it's important for traders to conduct thorough backtesting to evaluate the effectiveness of the settings in different market conditions.

- **Flexibility:** Traders should remain flexible and adjust MACD settings as market conditions evolve. Adapting MACD to specific market conditions requires ongoing analysis and adjustment to optimize trading performance.

# CHAPTER 13

# MACD AND VOLATILITY

Market volatility, characterized by rapid and unpredictable price movements, plays a significant role in shaping trading conditions and influencing the effectiveness of technical indicators like Moving Average Convergence Divergence (MACD). In this chapter, we will explore the relationship between MACD and market volatility, and discuss how traders can adjust their strategies to navigate both high and low volatility environments effectively.

**Understanding the Relationship between MACD and Market Volatility:**

MACD is a trend-following momentum indicator that measures the relationship between two moving averages, typically the 12-period and 26-period exponential moving averages. The behavior of MACD can be influenced by changes in market volatility in the following ways:

1. **Impact on Signal Sensitivity:** In high volatility environments, price swings tend to be larger and more frequent, leading to

increased noise in the market. As a result, MACD signals may become less reliable, as fluctuations in price can trigger false signals and whipsaws. Conversely, in low volatility environments, price movements may be subdued, leading to fewer trading opportunities and potentially less significant MACD signals.

2. **Effect on Momentum Confirmation:** MACD measures the momentum of price movements, with increasing values indicating strengthening momentum and decreasing values indicating weakening momentum. In high volatility environments, momentum signals on MACD may be more pronounced and exaggerated, reflecting the heightened market activity. In contrast, in low volatility environments, momentum signals may be more subdued and less reliable due to the lack of strong price movements.

**Adjusting Strategies for High and Low Volatility Environments:**

Traders can adjust their MACD strategies to adapt to both high and low volatility environments and capitalize on market opportunities effectively. Here are some considerations for adjusting strategies based on market volatility:

1. **High Volatility Environments:**

   - **Use Longer-Term Settings:** In high volatility environments, using longer-term settings for MACD can help smooth out noise and filter false signals. Traders may opt for longer-term moving averages (e.g., 26-period and 50-period EMAs) to capture broader trends and reduce the impact of short-term price fluctuations.

   - **Focus on Trend Confirmation:** Traders should prioritize trend confirmation signals on MACD in high volatility environments to avoid getting caught in false breakouts or breakdowns. Waiting for strong convergence or divergence signals on MACD, accompanied by increasing histogram bars, can provide more reliable indications of trend direction.

2. **Low Volatility Environments:**

- **Use Shorter-Term Settings:** In low volatility environments, using shorter-term settings for MACD can help capture smaller price movements and identify potential trading opportunities. Traders may opt for shorter-term moving averages (e.g., 5-period and 10-period EMAs) to generate more responsive signals and adapt quickly to changing market conditions.

- **Focus on Momentum Confirmation:** Traders should focus on momentum confirmation signals on MACD in low volatility environments to identify potential trend reversals or continuations. Paying attention to changes in histogram bars and the slope of the MACD line can provide valuable insights into shifts in market sentiment.

**Key Considerations:**

- **Adaptability:** Traders should remain adaptable and adjust their MACD strategies dynamically based on changing market conditions and volatility levels.

- **Risk Management:** Regardless of market volatility, proper risk management is essential to protect capital and mitigate potential losses. Traders should always use stop-loss orders and position sizing techniques to manage risk effectively.

# CHAPTER 14

# MACD AND FIBONACCI RETRACEMENTS

Integrating Moving Average Convergence Divergence (MACD) with Fibonacci retracement levels can provide traders with a powerful combination of technical analysis tools for identifying precise entries and exits in the market. In this chapter, we will explore how MACD can be combined with Fibonacci retracements to enhance trading strategies and improve trading accuracy.

**Integrating MACD with Fibonacci Retracement Levels:**

Fibonacci retracement levels are key technical levels derived from the Fibonacci sequence that are used to identify potential support and resistance levels in a market. These levels are commonly used by traders to anticipate price reversals or continuations. When combined with MACD, Fibonacci retracements can provide additional confirmation and validation of trading signals. Here's how:

1. **Identifying Key Retracement Levels:** Traders use Fibonacci retracement levels, such as the 38.2%, 50%, and 61.8% levels, to identify potential support and resistance levels in a market. These levels are derived from the Fibonacci sequence and are believed to represent areas where price is likely to reverse or consolidate.

2. **Confirming with MACD Signals:** Once key Fibonacci retracement levels are identified, traders can use MACD to confirm the validity of these levels. For example, a bullish divergence signal on MACD, accompanied by price bouncing off a Fibonacci support level, provides additional confirmation of a potential trend reversal.

3. **Aligning Signals for Entries and Exits:** By aligning MACD signals with Fibonacci retracement levels, traders can identify precise entry and exit points in the market. For example, a bullish crossover of the MACD line above the signal line, accompanied by price bouncing off a Fibonacci support level, may signal a strong buying opportunity.

**Combining Two Powerful Tools for Precise Entries and Exits:**

Combining MACD with Fibonacci retracements allows traders to leverage the strengths of both technical analysis tools for more precise entries and exits. Here are some benefits of this combination:

1. **Enhanced Confirmation:** By confirming MACD signals with Fibonacci retracement levels, traders can increase the confidence in their trading decisions. This combination provides multiple layers of confirmation, reducing the likelihood of false signals.

2. **Improved Precision:** The combination of MACD and Fibonacci retracements helps traders identify precise entry and exit points in the market. Traders can use Fibonacci levels to define

support and resistance zones, while MACD provides confirmation of momentum and trend direction.

3. **Better Risk Management:** Integrating MACD with Fibonacci retracements allows traders to implement more effective risk management strategies. Traders can use Fibonacci levels to set stop-loss orders and target profit levels, while MACD signals help in timing entries and exits.

## Key Considerations:

- **Backtesting:** Before incorporating MACD and Fibonacci retracements into live trading, it's essential for traders to conduct thorough backtesting to evaluate the effectiveness of this combination in different market conditions.

- **Market Context:** Traders should consider market context and other technical factors when using MACD and Fibonacci retracements. It's important to analyze price action, volume, and other indicators to confirm signals and avoid false positives.

# CHAPTER 15

# MACD AND ELLIOTT WAVE THEORY

Elliott Wave Theory is a popular technical analysis approach that seeks to identify recurring patterns in financial markets, known as Elliott waves. These waves represent the natural rhythm of market movements and are believed to follow specific rules and guidelines. In this chapter, we will explore how Moving Average Convergence Divergence (MACD) can be harmonized with Elliott Wave Theory to enhance wave counting and trend identification.

**Harmonizing MACD with Elliott Wave Patterns:**

Elliott Wave Theory identifies two types of waves: impulsive waves, which move in the direction of the trend, and corrective waves, which move against the trend. MACD can be used to confirm and validate Elliott wave patterns by providing additional insight into momentum and trend strength. Here's how:

1. **Confirming Impulsive Waves:** Impulsive waves are characterized by strong directional movement in the direction of the trend. Traders can use MACD to confirm the strength of

impulsive waves by analyzing the momentum and velocity of price movements. A bullish crossover of the MACD line above the signal line, accompanied by increasing histogram bars, can confirm the strength of an impulsive uptrend.

2. **Identifying Corrective Waves:** Corrective waves are characterized by sideways or countertrend movements that retrace a portion of the preceding impulsive wave. MACD can help traders identify potential reversal points and trend changes during corrective waves. For example, a bearish divergence signal on MACD, accompanied by decreasing histogram bars, may signal the end of a corrective rally and the resumption of the downtrend.

3. **Enhancing Wave Counting:** Elliott Wave Theory involves counting and labeling waves according to specific rules and guidelines. MACD can help traders validate wave counts by providing confirmation of trend direction and momentum. Traders can look for alignment between MACD signals and Elliott wave patterns to increase the accuracy of wave counting.

## Enhancing Wave Counting and Trend Identification:

By harmonizing MACD with Elliott Wave Theory, traders can enhance wave counting and trend identification in the following ways:

1. **Confirmation of Wave Structure:** MACD can help traders confirm the structure of Elliott waves by providing additional confirmation of trend direction and momentum. Traders can use MACD signals to validate wave counts and increase confidence in their analysis.

2. **Identification of Trend Reversals:** MACD can help traders identify potential trend reversals during corrective waves, allowing them to anticipate changes in market direction and

position themselves accordingly. Traders can use divergence signals on MACD to identify potential reversal points and adjust their trading strategy accordingly.

3. **Validation of Trend Strength:** MACD can help traders assess the strength of trends by analyzing the momentum and velocity of price movements. Increasing histogram bars and bullish/bearish crossovers on MACD can confirm the strength of impulsive waves and provide guidance on trend continuation.

## Key Considerations:

- **Practice and Experience:** Harmonizing MACD with Elliott Wave Theory requires practice and experience. Traders should familiarize themselves with both technical analysis approaches and understand how they complement each other in market analysis.

- **Risk Management:** Proper risk management is essential when trading based on Elliott Wave Theory and MACD signals. Traders should use stop-loss orders and position sizing techniques to manage risk effectively and protect capital.

# CHAPTER 16

# MACD AND SECTOR ROTATION

Sector rotation is a strategy employed by investors and traders to capitalize on the cyclical nature of different sectors within the market. By rotating positions based on sector strength, traders aim to outperform the broader market and maximize returns. In this chapter, we will explore how Moving Average Convergence Divergence (MACD) can be utilized to identify sector trends and facilitate sector rotation strategies.

**Using MACD to Identify Sector Trends:**

MACD can be an effective tool for identifying sector trends by analyzing the momentum and direction of price movements within specific sectors. Here's how traders can use MACD to identify sector trends:

1. **Sector ETF Analysis:** Traders can analyze sector-specific exchange-traded funds (ETFs) using MACD to identify trends and momentum shifts within different sectors of the market.

By applying MACD to sector ETF charts, traders can gain insights into sector rotation opportunities.

2. **Comparative Analysis:** Traders can compare the performance of different sectors using MACD to identify sectors exhibiting relative strength or weakness. By comparing MACD signals across sector ETFs, traders can identify sectors with bullish momentum and potential trading opportunities.

3. **Divergence Analysis:** MACD divergence signals can provide early indications of potential trend reversals or shifts in sector momentum. Traders can analyze MACD divergence between sector ETFs and broader market indices to identify sectors diverging from the overall market trend.

**Rotating Positions Based on Sector Strength:**

Once sector trends are identified using MACD, traders can implement sector rotation strategies to capitalize on relative strength and weakness within different sectors. Here's how traders can rotate positions based on sector strength:

1. **Trend Following:** Traders can allocate capital to sectors exhibiting strong bullish momentum, as confirmed by MACD signals. By focusing on sectors with rising MACD lines, bullish crossovers, and expanding histogram bars, traders can position themselves to benefit from trending sectors.

2. **Risk Management:** Traders should manage risk by diversifying across sectors and using stop-loss orders to limit downside risk. By rotating positions based on sector strength, traders can reduce exposure to underperforming sectors and mitigate portfolio risk.

3. **Monitoring Market Breadth:** Traders should monitor market breadth indicators, such as the percentage of sectors trading

above their moving averages, to gauge overall market health. By aligning sector rotation strategies with market breadth analysis and MACD signals, traders can make more informed decisions.

## Key Considerations:

- **Periodic Review:** Traders should periodically review sector rotation strategies to adapt to changing market conditions and sector dynamics. By continuously monitoring sector trends using MACD, traders can optimize sector allocation and maximize returns.

- **Economic Analysis:** Traders should consider economic factors and industry trends when implementing sector rotation strategies. By aligning sector allocation with broader economic themes and sector-specific catalysts, traders can capitalize on emerging opportunities.

# CHAPTER 17

# STATISTICAL ANALYSIS OF MACD STRATEGIES

Backtesting is a crucial step in evaluating the effectiveness of trading strategies, including those based on Moving Average Convergence Divergence (MACD). By conducting statistical analysis of MACD strategies, traders can assess performance, measure risk, and gain insights into the robustness of their trading approach. In this chapter, we will explore the process of backtesting MACD strategies and evaluating performance and risk metrics.

**Backtesting MACD Strategies:**

Backtesting involves testing a trading strategy using historical data to assess its performance under various market conditions. When backtesting MACD strategies, traders follow these steps:

1. **Data Collection:** Gather historical price data for the asset or market being analyzed. This data should include open, high, low, and close prices, as well as volume data.

2. **Strategy Definition:** Define the MACD strategy being tested, including entry and exit rules, position sizing, and risk management parameters.

3. **Implementation:** Implement the MACD strategy using trading software or programming languages such as Python or R. This involves coding the strategy logic and applying it to historical data.

4. **Testing Period:** Select a testing period, typically several years of historical data, to evaluate the performance of the MACD strategy.

5. **Analysis:** Analyze the results of the backtest, including performance metrics, equity curves, drawdowns, and trade statistics.

**Evaluating Performance and Risk Metrics:**

Several performance and risk metrics can be used to evaluate the effectiveness of MACD strategies. These metrics provide insights into profitability, risk exposure, and overall trading performance. Here are some key metrics to consider:

1. **Profitability Metrics:**

   - **Total Return:** The total percentage return generated by the strategy over the testing period.

   - **Annualized Return:** The average annual percentage return of the strategy.

- **Win Rate:** The percentage of winning trades out of total trades.

2. **Risk Metrics:**

   - **Drawdown:** The peak-to-trough decline in equity during the testing period.

   - **Risk-Adjusted Return:** Measures such as the Sharpe ratio or Sortino ratio, which adjust returns for the level of risk taken.

   - **Maximum Drawdown:** The largest percentage decline in equity from a peak to a trough.

3. **Trade Statistics:**

   - **Average Profit/Loss per Trade:** The average profit or loss generated per trade.

   - **Average Holding Period:** The average duration of trades in terms of bars or days.

   - **Trade Frequency:** The number of trades executed during the testing period.

## Interpreting Results and Iterating:

After conducting statistical analysis of MACD strategies, traders should interpret the results and consider potential adjustments or refinements to the strategy. This may involve optimizing parameters, adding filters, or incorporating additional indicators for confirmation. Iterative testing and refinement are essential to develop robust and adaptive trading strategies.

## Key Considerations:

- **Out-of-Sample Testing:** After conducting initial backtests, traders should perform out-of-sample testing to validate the robustness of the strategy on unseen data.

- **Realistic Assumptions:** Ensure that backtests are conducted using realistic assumptions, including transaction costs, slippage, and liquidity constraints.

- **Risk Management:** Consider the risk implications of the strategy and ensure that risk management measures are integrated into the trading approach.

# CHAPTER 18

# AUTOMATION WITH MACD

Automation has become increasingly prevalent in the world of trading, offering traders the ability to execute strategies with speed, precision, and efficiency. Moving Average Convergence Divergence (MACD), with its versatile applications in technical analysis, can be effectively integrated into automated trading algorithms. In this chapter, we will explore the process of creating and implementing MACD-based trading algorithms and discuss the benefits of automation for enhancing trading efficiency.

**Creating and Implementing MACD-Based Trading Algorithms:**

Creating a MACD-based trading algorithm involves defining specific rules and criteria for entry, exit, position sizing, and risk management. Here's a step-by-step guide to creating and implementing such an algorithm:

1. **Strategy Development:** Define the MACD strategy, including entry and exit rules, parameters for MACD calculation, signal generation, and trade execution. Consider factors such as trend identification, momentum confirmation, and risk management.

2. **Coding the Algorithm:** Translate the MACD strategy into code using a programming language such as Python, R, or a proprietary trading platform's scripting language. Implement logic for MACD calculations, signal generation, trade execution, and position management.

3. **Backtesting:** Backtest the MACD-based algorithm using historical data to evaluate its performance under various market conditions. Assess profitability, risk metrics, and trade statistics to validate the effectiveness of the strategy.

4. **Optimization:** Fine-tune the parameters of the MACD strategy through optimization techniques such as parameter sweeps, genetic algorithms, or machine learning algorithms. Aim to maximize profitability and robustness while minimizing risk.

5. **Out-of-Sample Testing:** Validate the performance of the optimized algorithm on out-of-sample data to ensure its effectiveness on unseen market data. Verify that the strategy remains robust and adaptive across different market environments.

6. **Deployment:** Deploy the automated trading algorithm in live or simulated trading environments, monitoring its performance in real-time. Implement risk management measures and monitoring tools to ensure the algorithm operates within predefined parameters.

**Incorporating Automation for Efficiency:**

Automation offers several benefits for traders utilizing MACD-based strategies:

1. **Speed and Efficiency:** Automated trading algorithms can execute trades with speed and precision, reacting to market conditions in real-time. This allows traders to capitalize on opportunities quickly and efficiently.

2. **Emotion-Free Trading:** Automation eliminates emotional biases and human errors from trading decisions, ensuring consistency and discipline in strategy execution. This can lead to improved trading performance and reduced psychological stress.

3. **24/7 Market Coverage:** Automated trading algorithms can operate continuously, providing 24/7 market coverage across different time zones and trading sessions. This allows traders to capture opportunities even when they are unable to monitor the markets actively.

4. **Scalability:** Automated trading algorithms can be scaled to handle large volumes of trades and multiple markets simultaneously. This scalability enables traders to expand their trading operations and diversify their portfolios efficiently.

## Key Considerations:

- **Risk Management:** Implement robust risk management measures in automated trading algorithms to protect capital and minimize losses. This may include setting stop-loss orders, position sizing rules, and portfolio diversification strategies.

- **Monitoring and Oversight:** Continuously monitor the performance of automated trading algorithms and intervene if necessary to address any issues or anomalies. Regularly review and update the algorithm to adapt to changing market conditions.

- **Regulatory Compliance:** Ensure compliance with regulatory requirements and guidelines when deploying automated trading algorithms. Adhere to best practices for algorithmic trading and maintain transparency in trading activities.

# CHAPTER 19

# MACD IN OPTIONS TRADING

Options trading offers traders the opportunity to profit from price movements in financial assets with limited risk exposure. Moving Average Convergence Divergence (MACD), a versatile technical indicator, can be effectively leveraged in options trading to identify trends, generate trading signals, and manage risk. In this chapter, we will explore how MACD can be integrated into options trading strategies and discuss its role in hedging and risk management.

**Leveraging MACD for Options Strategies:**

MACD can be applied to various options trading strategies, including directional trades, volatility plays, and income-generating strategies. Here's how MACD can be leveraged in different options strategies:

1. **Directional Trades:** Traders can use MACD to identify directional trends in underlying assets and select appropriate options strategies based on trend direction. For example, if MACD indicates a bullish trend, traders may consider buying

call options or selling put options to profit from upward price movements.

2. **Volatility Plays:** MACD can help traders assess changes in market volatility and adjust options strategies accordingly. For example, increasing volatility, as indicated by widening histogram bars on MACD, may prompt traders to employ straddle or strangle strategies to capitalize on potential price swings.

3. **Income-Generating Strategies:** MACD can be used in conjunction with options selling strategies, such as covered calls or cash-secured puts, to generate income while managing risk. Traders can use MACD signals to time entries and exits for options positions, enhancing profitability and risk-adjusted returns.

**Hedging and Risk Management with MACD:**

In options trading, risk management is crucial for preserving capital and mitigating losses. MACD can play a role in hedging and risk management strategies by providing insights into trend strength, momentum, and market sentiment. Here's how MACD can be used for hedging and risk management:

1. **Trend Confirmation:** MACD can help traders confirm the direction of the underlying trend, allowing them to align options positions accordingly. For example, traders may hedge long options positions with protective puts or short options positions with covered calls based on MACD signals.

2. **Timing Entries and Exits:** MACD signals can be used to time entries and exits for options positions, optimizing trade execution and minimizing risk exposure. Traders may initiate options positions when MACD indicates a strong trend

confirmation and exit positions when MACD signals a potential trend reversal.

3. **Dynamic Position Adjustment:** MACD can be used to monitor market conditions and adjust options positions dynamically in response to changing trends and volatility levels. Traders may roll options positions, adjust strike prices, or change expiration dates based on MACD signals to adapt to evolving market dynamics.

## Key Considerations:

- **Parameter Selection:** Traders should optimize MACD parameters (e.g., fast and slow EMA periods, signal line period) based on the characteristics of the underlying asset and the desired trading timeframe.

- **Risk Assessment:** Evaluate the risk-reward profile of options strategies and assess potential losses before entering trades. Implement risk management measures, such as position sizing and stop-loss orders, to limit downside risk.

- **Continuous Monitoring:** Continuously monitor MACD signals and market conditions to adapt options strategies as needed. Remain vigilant for changes in trend direction, volatility levels, and other factors that may impact options positions.

# CHAPTER 20

# PSYCHOLOGICAL ASPECTS OF MACD TRADING

Successful trading with Moving Average Convergence Divergence (MACD) isn't just about understanding technical analysis or having a solid strategy; it also requires managing the psychological aspects of trading. In this chapter, we'll delve into the psychological aspects of MACD trading, including how to manage emotions effectively, develop discipline, and cultivate patience.

**Managing Emotions while Trading with MACD:**

Trading can evoke a range of emotions, including fear, greed, anxiety, and excitement. These emotions can cloud judgment and lead to impulsive decision-making, which can negatively impact trading performance. Here's how traders can manage emotions while trading with MACD:

1. **Stay Objective:** Focus on the signals generated by MACD rather than letting emotions dictate trading decisions. Stick to

your trading plan and avoid making impulsive trades based on fear or greed.

2. **Control Risk:** Implement proper risk management techniques, such as setting stop-loss orders and position sizing, to limit potential losses. Knowing that you have a plan in place can help alleviate anxiety and reduce emotional stress.

3. **Practice Mindfulness:** Stay present and aware of your thoughts and emotions while trading. Mindfulness techniques, such as deep breathing or visualization, can help calm the mind and maintain focus during volatile market conditions.

**Developing Discipline and Patience:**

Discipline and patience are essential traits for successful trading with MACD. Here's how traders can cultivate these qualities:

1. **Stick to Your Plan:** Develop a trading plan based on MACD signals and stick to it consistently. Avoid deviating from your plan or chasing trades based on impulse.

2. **Be Patient:** Wait for high-probability setups and confirmation from MACD before entering trades. Patience is key to avoiding overtrading and waiting for the right opportunities to present themselves.

3. **Review and Learn:** Continuously review your trades and analyze your performance with MACD. Learn from both successes and failures, and use this knowledge to refine your trading approach over time.

**Mindset Shift:**

Shift your mindset from focusing solely on profits to prioritizing the process and consistency. Understand that losses are a natural part of trading and focus on executing your strategy with discipline and patience.

**Visualization and Affirmations:**

Visualize successful trades and affirm positive beliefs about your trading abilities. Visualization and positive affirmations can help reinforce confidence and overcome self-doubt.

**Seek Support:**

Connect with other traders, mentors, or trading communities to share experiences and gain insights. Having a support network can provide encouragement and accountability in your trading journey.

**Key Takeaways:**

- Emotions can impact trading decisions, so it's essential to stay objective and control risk.

- Discipline and patience are crucial for successful trading with MACD. Stick to your plan and wait for high-probability setups.

- Develop a mindset focused on process and consistency, and use visualization and positive affirmations to reinforce confidence.

- Seek support from other traders or mentors to stay motivated and accountable in your trading journey.

# CHAPTER 21

# REAL-WORLD EXAMPLES

In this chapter, we'll explore real-world examples of successful trades using Moving Average Convergence Divergence (MACD). By examining both winning and losing trades, traders can gain valuable insights into the application of MACD in different market conditions and learn from practical experiences.

**Case Study 1: Bullish MACD Crossover**

*Market Context:*

- Asset: XYZ stock

- Timeframe: Daily chart

- MACD Setup: 12-period EMA, 26-period EMA, 9-period signal line

- Trade Type: Long (Buy)

*Trade Execution:*

1. MACD Line Crosses Above Signal Line: On April 1st, the MACD line crosses above the signal line, indicating a bullish crossover.

2. Confirmation of Trend: The histogram bars start to increase, confirming the strength of the bullish momentum.

3. Entry: Traders enter a long position in XYZ stock at the open of the next trading day (April 2nd).

4. Trade Management: A trailing stop-loss order is placed below recent swing lows to protect profits.

*Outcome:*

- XYZ stock experiences a sustained uptrend following the MACD crossover.

- Traders exit the position when the MACD line crosses below the signal line, signaling a potential trend reversal.

- Profit: 15% gain on the trade.

## Case Study 2: Bearish MACD Divergence

*Market Context:*

- Asset: ABC stock

- Timeframe: 4-hour chart

- MACD Setup: 12-period EMA, 26-period EMA, 9-period signal line

- Trade Type: Short (Sell)

*Trade Execution:*

1. MACD Divergence: On June 15th, ABC stock makes a new high, but the MACD histogram shows decreasing bars, indicating bearish divergence.

2. Confirmation of Weakness: The MACD line starts to slope downwards, confirming weakening momentum.

3. Entry: Traders initiate a short position in ABC stock at the close of the trading day on June 15th.

4. Trade Management: A stop-loss order is placed above the recent swing high to manage risk.

*Outcome:*

- ABC stock enters a downtrend following the bearish divergence signal on MACD.

- Traders exit the position when the MACD line crosses above the signal line, indicating a potential trend reversal.

- Profit: 10% gain on the trade.

**Key Takeaways:**

1. MACD signals can be effectively applied across different timeframes and assets.

2. Confirmation of trend direction and momentum is crucial for trade execution.

3. Proper risk management, including stop-loss orders, helps protect capital in case of adverse price movements.

4. Learning from both successful and unsuccessful trades is essential for continuous improvement as a trader.

# CHAPTER 22

# COMMON MISTAKES IN MACD TRADING

In this chapter, we'll explore common mistakes that traders make when using Moving Average Convergence Divergence (MACD) and provide insights into how to avoid these pitfalls. By identifying and addressing these mistakes, traders can fine-tune their strategies and improve their trading results with MACD.

## 1. Overlooking Market Context:

*Mistake:* Failing to consider broader market context, such as economic indicators, news events, and overall market sentiment, before relying solely on MACD signals.

*Solution:* Always analyze market context in conjunction with MACD signals. Consider factors that may impact price movements and use MACD as a confirmation tool rather than a standalone indicator.

## 2. Ignoring Signal Confirmation:

*Mistake:* Taking MACD signals at face value without seeking confirmation from other technical indicators or price action.

*Solution:* Confirm MACD signals with other technical indicators, such as volume, trendlines, or support/resistance levels, to validate trading decisions. Look for convergence of signals to increase confidence in trade setups.

### 3. Chasing Signals:

*Mistake:* Entering trades impulsively based on fleeting MACD signals without waiting for confirmation or proper setup.

*Solution:* Exercise patience and discipline when trading with MACD. Wait for high-probability setups with clear confirmation signals before entering trades, and avoid chasing price movements.

### 4. Neglecting Risk Management:

*Mistake:* Failing to implement proper risk management techniques, such as setting stop-loss orders or position sizing, which can lead to significant losses.

*Solution:* Always prioritize risk management when trading with MACD. Use stop-loss orders to limit potential losses and position sizing to manage risk exposure effectively.

### 5. Over-Optimization:

*Mistake:* Tweaking MACD parameters excessively to fit historical data, leading to over-optimization and unrealistic performance expectations.

*Solution:* Avoid over-optimization by using reasonable MACD parameters and testing strategies on out-of-sample data to ensure robustness across different market conditions.

### 6. Lack of Adaptability:

*Mistake:* Relying on a single MACD strategy without adapting to changing market conditions or incorporating new information.

*Solution:* Remain flexible and adaptable in your approach to MACD trading. Continuously monitor market dynamics and adjust strategies as needed to stay ahead of evolving trends.

## 7. Emotional Trading:

*Mistake:* Allowing emotions such as fear, greed, or impatience to influence trading decisions, leading to irrational behavior and poor outcomes.

*Solution:* Develop emotional discipline and resilience when trading with MACD. Stick to your trading plan, manage risk effectively, and avoid making impulsive decisions based on emotions.

## Key Takeaways:

- Market context is crucial for interpreting MACD signals accurately.

- Confirm MACD signals with other technical indicators or price action patterns.

- Exercise patience and discipline; avoid chasing signals or over-trading.

- Prioritize risk management to protect capital and minimize losses.

- Avoid over-optimization and remain adaptable to changing market conditions.

- Control emotions and maintain emotional discipline when trading with MACD.

# CHAPTER 23

# MACD IN CRYPTOCURRENCY TRADING

Cryptocurrency markets are known for their volatility and unique characteristics, presenting both opportunities and challenges for traders. In this chapter, we'll explore how Moving Average Convergence Divergence (MACD) can be adapted to the cryptocurrency market and discuss strategies for trading digital assets effectively.

**Adapting MACD to the Cryptocurrency Market:**

The principles of MACD remain applicable in cryptocurrency trading, but certain adaptations may be necessary due to the unique characteristics of digital asset markets:

1. **Volatility Consideration:** Cryptocurrency markets are often more volatile than traditional markets, leading to faster price movements. Adjusting MACD parameters, such as shortening

the moving average periods, can help capture shorter-term trends in cryptocurrency prices.

2. **Liquidity Assessment:** Liquidity can vary significantly across different cryptocurrencies, impacting price action and the reliability of MACD signals. Focus on trading cryptocurrencies with sufficient liquidity to ensure accurate price discovery and smoother market execution.

3. **24/7 Trading Environment:** Cryptocurrency markets operate 24/7, unlike traditional markets that have specific trading hours. Consider using MACD signals on different timeframes to adapt to the continuous nature of cryptocurrency trading.

**Strategies for Trading Digital Assets:**

Several MACD-based strategies can be employed in cryptocurrency trading:

1. **Trend Following:** Use MACD crossovers to identify trends in cryptocurrency prices and initiate trades in the direction of the trend. Look for bullish crossovers (MACD line crossing above the signal line) for buy signals and bearish crossovers (MACD line crossing below the signal line) for sell signals.

2. **Divergence Analysis:** Apply MACD divergence analysis to identify potential trend reversals or shifts in cryptocurrency prices. Look for divergences between MACD and price action to anticipate changes in market direction.

3. **Volatility Trading:** Utilize MACD histogram patterns to gauge changes in volatility and trade cryptocurrency breakouts or breakdowns accordingly. Increasing histogram bars may indicate rising volatility, while decreasing bars may signal decreasing volatility.

**Risk Management:**

Risk management is paramount in cryptocurrency trading due to the inherent volatility and uncertainty in digital asset markets. Implement the following risk management practices:

- Use stop-loss orders to limit potential losses and protect capital.

- Diversify your cryptocurrency portfolio to spread risk across different assets.

- Avoid overleveraging positions, as cryptocurrency markets can experience rapid price movements.

## Key Considerations:

- Stay informed about developments in the cryptocurrency space, including regulatory changes, technological advancements, and market sentiment.

- Continuously monitor MACD signals and adapt strategies to changing market conditions.

- Test MACD strategies on historical cryptocurrency data and conduct thorough backtesting before trading live.

## Conclusion:

Adapting MACD to cryptocurrency trading requires an understanding of the unique characteristics of digital asset markets. By employing MACD-based strategies tailored to cryptocurrency trading, traders can capitalize on opportunities while managing risks effectively. With proper risk management and continuous monitoring of MACD signals, traders can navigate the dynamic cryptocurrency market with confidence and achieve success in their trading endeavors.

# CHAPTER 24

# FUTURE DEVELOPMENTS IN MACD

Moving Average Convergence Divergence (MACD) has been a staple technical indicator for traders for decades, but the field of technical analysis is ever-evolving. In this chapter, we'll explore recent advancements in MACD analysis and speculate on potential future innovations and improvements.

**Recent Advancements in MACD Analysis:**

1. **Machine Learning Integration:** Some traders and researchers are exploring the integration of machine learning algorithms with MACD analysis. Machine learning models can help identify complex patterns in MACD signals and improve predictive accuracy.

2. **Dynamic Parameter Optimization:** Traditional MACD parameters (e.g., 12, 26, 9) are static and may not always adapt well to changing market conditions. Recent advancements involve dynamic parameter optimization techniques that

adjust MACD parameters based on market volatility, trend strength, or other factors.

3. **Multi-Timeframe Analysis:** Traders are increasingly using MACD signals across multiple timeframes to gain a more comprehensive view of market trends and improve trade timing. Advanced techniques involve integrating MACD signals from different timeframes to generate more robust trading signals.

4. **Sentiment Analysis:** Incorporating sentiment analysis into MACD analysis is gaining traction. By analyzing social media sentiment, news sentiment, or market sentiment indicators alongside MACD signals, traders can gain insights into market psychology and improve decision-making.

## Potential Future Innovations and Improvements:

1. **Adaptive MACD:** Future developments may involve the creation of adaptive MACD indicators that automatically adjust parameters based on market conditions. Adaptive MACD could dynamically respond to changes in volatility, trend duration, and other factors to generate more accurate signals.

2. **Deep Learning Applications:** Deep learning techniques, such as recurrent neural networks (RNNs) and convolutional neural networks (CNNs), hold promise for advancing MACD analysis. Deep learning models can learn complex patterns in MACD data and identify subtle signals that may be overlooked by traditional methods.

3. **Quantum Computing:** As quantum computing technology advances, it may offer new possibilities for analyzing MACD data at unprecedented speeds. Quantum computing could enable more complex analysis of large datasets and enhance the accuracy of MACD-based predictions.

4. **Interdisciplinary Research:** Future developments in MACD analysis may benefit from interdisciplinary research collaborations, involving experts from fields such as mathematics, computer science, finance, and psychology. Collaborative efforts could lead to innovative approaches and breakthroughs in MACD analysis.

## Challenges and Considerations:

1. **Data Quality:** High-quality data is essential for accurate MACD analysis. Ensuring data integrity and addressing issues such as data gaps, outliers, and noise are critical for reliable results.

2. **Model Interpretability:** As MACD analysis becomes more sophisticated, ensuring model interpretability and transparency becomes increasingly important. Traders should be able to understand how MACD signals are generated and interpret their implications for trading decisions.

3. **Ethical Considerations:** Ethical considerations, such as privacy, fairness, and bias, should be addressed in MACD analysis. Traders and researchers must adhere to ethical standards and consider the societal impact of their work.

## Conclusion:

The future of MACD analysis holds exciting possibilities, with advancements in machine learning, adaptive algorithms, and interdisciplinary research pushing the boundaries of technical analysis. By staying informed about recent developments and embracing innovation, traders can leverage the power of MACD analysis to gain a competitive edge in the dynamic and evolving financial markets of the future.

# CHAPTER 25

# CONCLUSION

In this book, we've delved deep into the world of Moving Average Convergence Divergence (MACD) and explored its applications in trading across various markets and conditions. As we conclude our journey, let's summarize the key takeaways and emphasize the importance of ongoing learning and adaptation in the pursuit of trading success.

**Key Takeaways:**

1. **Versatility of MACD:** MACD is a versatile technical indicator that can be applied to various trading strategies, including trend following, momentum trading, and reversal patterns.

2. **Signal Interpretation:** Understanding MACD signals, including crossovers, divergences, and histogram patterns, is essential for making informed trading decisions.

3. **Risk Management:** Prioritizing risk management through proper position sizing, stop-loss orders, and portfolio

diversification is crucial for protecting capital and minimizing losses.

4. **Psychological Discipline:** Embracing emotional discipline, patience, and resilience is fundamental for successful trading with MACD, helping traders navigate the ups and downs of the markets with confidence.

5. **Continuous Improvement:** Learning from both successes and failures, adapting strategies to changing market conditions, and staying abreast of advancements in MACD analysis are essential for continuous improvement as a trader.

**Encouraging Ongoing Learning and Adaptation:**

Trading is an ever-evolving field, and success requires a commitment to ongoing learning and adaptation. As you continue your trading journey, remember the following:

1. **Stay Curious:** Remain curious and open to new ideas, strategies, and technologies in trading. The willingness to explore and experiment can lead to breakthroughs and innovation.

2. **Embrace Challenges:** Embrace challenges and setbacks as opportunities for growth and learning. Every trade, win or loss, offers insights that can inform future decisions and improve trading performance.

3. **Seek Knowledge:** Continuously seek knowledge and education in trading, technical analysis, and market dynamics. Explore diverse perspectives and learn from experts, mentors, and fellow traders.

4. **Stay Flexible:** Adaptability is key to success in trading. Stay flexible and agile, adjusting strategies and tactics as needed to navigate changing market conditions and seize opportunities.

5. **Stay Disciplined:** Maintain discipline and consistency in your trading approach, adhering to your trading plan and risk management principles even in the face of uncertainty and volatility.

As you continue your trading journey with MACD and beyond, remember that success is not defined by individual trades or outcomes but by your commitment to learning, growth, and continuous improvement. By embracing the lessons learned in this book and remaining dedicated to your development as a trader, you can achieve your financial goals and thrive in the dynamic world of trading.

# APPENDIX

# TRADING EXERCISES

1. **Backtesting Exercise:**

   - Select a trading strategy based on MACD or any other indicator.

   - Apply the strategy to historical market data over a specific time period.

   - Analyze the performance of the strategy, including win rate, risk-adjusted returns, and drawdowns.

   - Identify strengths and weaknesses of the strategy and make adjustments accordingly.

2. **Paper Trading Exercise:**

   - Choose a trading strategy and simulate trades in real-time using paper trading or a trading simulator.

   - Record each trade, including entry and exit points, position size, and reasoning behind the trade.

- Review the performance of the simulated trades and assess the effectiveness of the strategy.

- Identify areas for improvement and refine the strategy based on the results.

3. **Risk Management Exercise:**

   - Calculate the optimal position size for a trade based on risk tolerance and account size.

   - Determine stop-loss levels for different trading scenarios to limit potential losses.

   - Evaluate the risk-reward ratio for potential trades and assess whether the risk justifies the potential reward.

   - Practice implementing risk management principles in simulated trades or live trading with small position sizes.

4. **Trade Journaling Exercise:**

   - Start a trade journal to record details of each trade, including entry and exit points, trade rationale, and emotional state.

   - Reflect on each trade and analyze the decision-making process, including strengths and areas for improvement.

   - Identify recurring patterns or mistakes in trading behavior and develop strategies to address them.

   - Review the trade journal regularly to track progress and measure performance over time.

5. **Market Analysis Exercise:**

- Conduct comprehensive market analysis using technical and fundamental analysis techniques.

- Identify key support and resistance levels, trend lines, and chart patterns on relevant market charts.

- Evaluate macroeconomic factors, news events, and sentiment indicators that may impact market movements.

- Develop a trading plan based on the analysis and identify potential trade setups with defined entry and exit criteria.

6. **Risk Simulation Exercise:**

- Use a position sizing calculator to simulate different trading scenarios and assess the impact of varying risk levels on portfolio performance.

- Experiment with different risk-reward ratios and position sizes to understand their effect on overall profitability and risk exposure.

- Analyze the results to determine the optimal balance between risk and reward for your trading strategy and risk tolerance.

7. **Emotional Control Exercise:**

- Practice mindfulness and emotional control techniques to manage emotions while trading.

- Before entering a trade, assess your emotional state and ensure you are in a calm and focused mindset.

- Implement strategies such as deep breathing, visualization, or positive affirmations to stay grounded and maintain discipline during volatile market conditions.

- Review each trade and reflect on how emotions may have influenced your decision-making process, identifying areas for improvement.

8. **Strategy Development Exercise:**

    - Experiment with developing your own trading strategy based on MACD or other technical indicators.

    - Define clear entry and exit criteria, position sizing rules, and risk management parameters for the strategy.

    - Backtest the strategy using historical market data to assess its performance and refine the parameters as needed.

    - Paper trade or simulate the strategy in real-time to evaluate its effectiveness in live market conditions.